Isle of Wight Cycle

Ten routes, with a mix of r
Graded, from easy to

www.iowcycleroutes.co.uk

Compiled and illustrated by Alan Rowe
First published in 2009, revised edition 2014.

The Long Stone, Mottistone.

CONTENTS

Cycling on the Island. 3
New to cycling. 4
How to use the guide. 5
The routes at a glance. 6-7
1. Yarmouth Estuary Excursion. 8
2. Merstone Meander. 12
3. A Ride with Sea-views. 15
4. The Newtown Navigator. 22

5. Bembridge Peninsula. 27
6. Wootton Tracks 'n' Trains. 34
7. South Wight Wander. 39
8. The Carisbrooke Canter. 46
9. The Brading Bash. 50
10. Brighstone Boneshaker. 56
Isle of Wight Cycling directory of shops, events etc. 62-64

INTRODUCTION

Cycling is currently enjoying a renaissance, and the proof is out there, on any sunny day you will see bikes of all varieties whizzing along, their riders sporting smiles and giving off a general air of happiness! Increasingly, joy is sometimes hard to find in a world full of serious preoccupations such as financial pressures, health worries or the state of the environment. Well, cycling has the cure! When you choose to travel by bike you have opted for a low cost, health enhancing occupation that has little or no impact on the natural world, and don't forget one of the best benefits... cycling is fun! There is no finer way of interacting with a landscape that, when viewed from a car, is little more than a blur. On a bike you become an explorer, The South Pole and the source of the Nile have already been found, but you can still experience the thrill of cresting a hill and discovering a beautiful vista that you have never seen before. On a smaller scale simply stop as you pass through an ancient wood, you may see a slow worm at your feet or notice a falling leaf dislodged by a Red Squirrel.

One of the world's great thinkers, Albert Einstein, was a keen cyclist, in fact he had most of his best ideas while pedalling along. He said "Life is like riding a bicycle, to keep your balance you must keep moving". Well, you don't have to be a genius to realise that cycling is the best way to keep fit while enjoying the great outdoors.

CYCLING ON THE ISLAND

The Isle of Wight has always been a popular holiday destination, and with good reason. Within a relatively small area you have all the elements required to enjoy a day out, bracing coastal scenery, gently rolling downland and charming villages nestling in a rural landscape. There are also resorts for those who hanker for amusement arcades and kiss-me-quick hats!

You will encounter hills, some big, some small, and having a thriving agricultural economy it's not unusual to turn a corner and find a tractor in your path or even a herd of cows! The road surfaces can vary in rural areas and in summer the traffic increases considerably (I told you it was a popular place), bear this in mind when travelling along the lanes. Many of the off-road routes take you on or near farmland so please take care to close any gates and treat animals with care and respect. There is a wonderful network of country lanes and with 165 miles of bridleways and 29 miles of byways you have the option to spend a lot of time on traffic free tracks. Riding on the Island is like reading a good book, once you have opened the pages you'll be hooked, and you'll want to read it again and again, always finding something you missed first time around.

Nippy, the cycling squirrel will pop up from time to time and ask a question! Try and answer before looking up the solutions on page 64!

3

NEW TO CYCLING?

Whether you are new to cycling or returning after a long absence, the key word is preparation. Don't be tempted to buy the first bike you see in a great rush of enthusiasm, you'll probably end up taking it back!

Spend some time thinking about the kind of riding you will do most often. Will you be cycling mostly on-road, off-road or a mixture of both? Bikes fall into 3 basic categories,

1. **Road Bikes.** Racing bikes with drop handlebars and thin wheels and lightweight touring bikes with mudguards and racks.

2. **Mountain Bikes.** Sturdy machines with straight handlebars and smaller wheels with chunky tyres, sometimes the frames and forks will have suspension.

3. **Hybrid Bikes.** As the name suggests, these have a combination of both, they will go well on the road and are rugged enough to take off-road.

Choosing the correct size of bike is vital for children and adults alike as it has a bearing on safe bike handling and comfort. As the types of frame vary so much it's not possible to give a size chart here but when you seek out your new bike stress to the retailer the importance of bike sizing (it's a good idea to go to the shop armed with your height and inside leg measurement). You don't need to spend thousands on a bike but if you are looking for something that will last more than a few months be prepared to spend £200 + and if you go for a second hand machine always get it serviced by a good bike shop or mobile service. If you are returning to cycling after a few years you may well have an old bike lurking in the dark recesses of the shed, again do get it serviced and expect to buy some new parts. An old bike may look OK after a quick clean but the brake cables could be brittle or the tyres can shrivel with age.

Recommended maps.
Ordnance Survey, **Explorer Map OL29**, 1:25,000.
Landranger Map, Sheet 196, 1:50,000.
Perry's Guide Maps of the Isle of Wight.

HOW TO USE THE GUIDE

The 10 routes have been roughly graded from easy to challenging in numerical order as they appear in the book. The first three routes in particular have options that will appeal to the young family. For example, on the Yarmouth route you can turn back at point 1 to have a flat, entirely traffic free ride, by contrast the Newtown ride is all on-road. Most of the rides have alternative routes, some to make your journey shorter, others to encourage you to see more sights such as The Duver on the Bembridge route. It's worth spending a few moments reading the Ride Overviews and studying the maps before choosing your route, also on pages 6/7 you will find all the routes 'at a glance' which will help with planning your day out. The distance of each ride doesn't necessarily indicate an easy ride, as off-roading is that much harder! The prompt points (see key below) give a more detailed description of complicated sections of the route. Abreviations are used such as L and R for turning left or right but the full word is used for bearing in either direction.

At the beginning of each ride you will see a long number like this SZ 35757 89357 these are the National Grid References of the ride start points.
www.gridreferencefinder.com

KEY TO ROUTE MAPS

● ● ● Main route.

o o o Alternative route.

●→ Route direction.

❸ Route prompts.

✪ Caution.

● ▶ Moderate climb.

● ▶▶ Steepish climb.

● ▶▶▶ Very steep climb.

● ▷ Descent.

〰 Roads.

〜 Track/bridleway.

– – – Bridleway.

- - - - Footpaths.

''''''' Route across open grassland.

S Route start.

Ⓐ Points of interest.

●—● Gate.

P Car park.

WC Toilet.

\|/ Viewpoint.

☕ Cafe.

🍺 Pub.

✗ Camping.

🏘 Buildings.

★ Information boards.

As you cycle round the routes you'll come across these signs.

They are blue and white and show the Round The Island Route, maintained by the Isle of Wight Council (see directory)

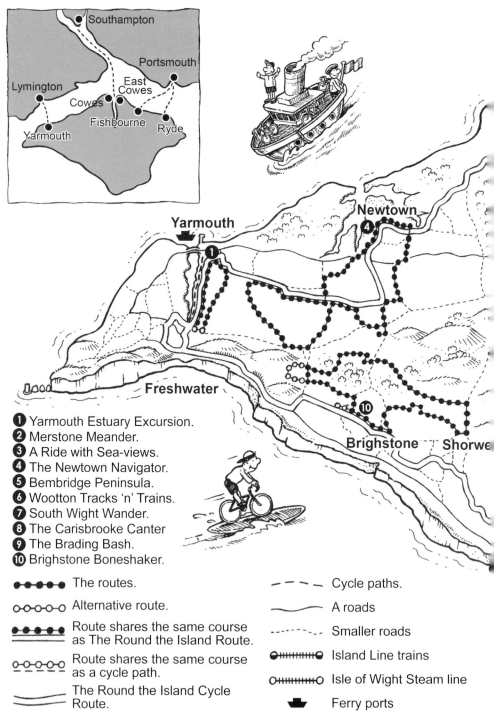

1 Yarmouth Estuary Excursion.
2 Merstone Meander.
3 A Ride with Sea-views.
4 The Newtown Navigator.
5 Bembridge Peninsula.
6 Wootton Tracks 'n' Trains.
7 South Wight Wander.
8 The Carisbrooke Canter
9 The Brading Bash.
10 Brighstone Boneshaker.

●●●●●	The routes.	– – – –	Cycle paths.
o-o-o-o-o	Alternative route.	————	A roads
●●●●● ————	Route shares the same course as The Round the Island Route.	··········	Smaller roads
o-o-o-o-o – – –	Route shares the same course as a cycle path.	O╫╫╫╫╫O	Island Line trains
————	The Round the Island Cycle Route.	O╫╫╫╫╫O	Isle of Wight Steam line
		⚓	Ferry ports

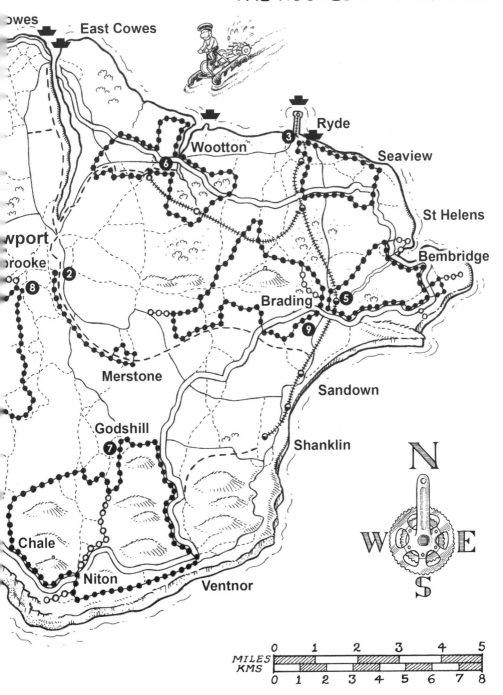

owes

East Cowes

Wootton

Ryde

Seaview

St Helens

Bembridge

wport

rooke

Brading

Merstone

Sandown

Godshill

Shanklin

Chale

Niton

Ventnor

N
W   E
S

MILES
KMS

0 1 2 3 4 5

0 1 2 3 4 5 6 7 8

7

This ride takes you through some lovely countryside and is predominately in an Area of Outstanding Natural Beauty (AONB). The first section of this route, from the start to point 1, is a traffic free bridleway used as a cycle path*, with a flat, stable gravel surface, and is ideal for young or inexperienced cyclists. From point 1 onwards it does include roads with light traffic and undulating gradients.

*The route to point 1 forms part of a network of cyclepaths maintained by the Isle of Wight Council. For more information on routes and events visit this web site www.sunseaandcycling.com

A selection of wading birds doing the 'River Dance' on the Yar Estuary mud!

Nippy Asks;
1. Can you identify the 4 wading birds above?

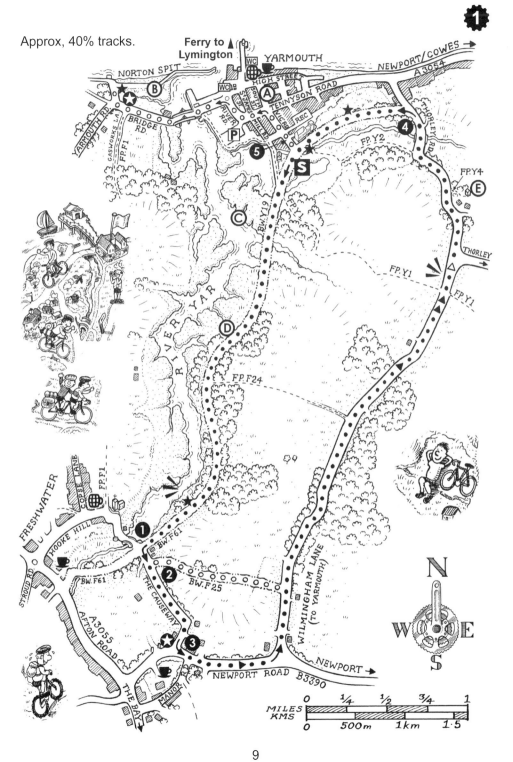

Approx, 40% tracks.

Start. Old Railway Station Yarmouth.

SZ 35757 89357

S Setting off from the former station (Cycle Hire and bistro/cafe), follow the sign 'Public Bridleway Y19 Freshwater 1 ¾ ' and proceed along the gravel track.

❶ *At this point if you are riding with young children or want a completely off-road, flat ride, you can turn back and retrace your wheel tracks back to the start to complete a 3.2 miles/5.1kms ride.*
To continue on the main route turn L at the bridge onto the tarmac road (sign showing a white Island on a blue background).

❷ *At around 100 yards/metres from the last left turn is an alternative off-road route (bridleway F25, wooden post) to Wilmingham Ln. The initial section of this track is quite muddy but gives way to a pleasant single track, with undulations, which will cut out a section of road. When the track meets the road turn L.*
If you want to stay on the main route proceed to the junction with the B3390.

❸ Turn L (sign to Newport, ignore the blue bicycle sign pointing right), take care, this is a main road, and take the next L into Wilmingham Lane (sign to Yarmouth A 3054). Stay on this road until point 4 just after the low stone bridge.

❹ Having crossed the bridge, continue for another 150 yards/metres, climb a slight hill and then turn L onto the track (bridleway Y19). There are some tall pine trees opposite and a couple of triangular road signs near the entrance to the track. You are now back on the old railway/cycle path and will soon see the former station.

❺ *An alternative route to Norton Spit.*
From the former station, cycle up the small slope onto the road and go straight ahead, do not turn off, and at the junction with Tennyson Rd (main road) turn L. Follow the road and at the roundabout, bear L, (signs for Totland, A3054) continue over the bridge and when you see Gasworks Lane on the left, pull in and stop (the next section of road has a potentially dangerous bend so I advise walking with your bike from here, it's not far). Cross the road (when it's safe) over to the black metal gates opposite and walk along the pavement. At the corner turn R (sign, footpath) and you'll soon be on Norton Spit. To return to the start simply retrace your steps.

POINTS OF INTEREST

Ⓐ The Town Of Yarmouth.

This pretty coastal town abounds with interesting shops, cafes and pubs, ideal for the curious, hungry and thirsty cyclist. Why not promenade along the pier, or visit Yarmouth Castle, built by Henry VIII in 1547.

Ⓑ Norton Spit.

This site of special scientific interest (SSSI) provides protection for the Western Yar estuary and allows the salt marsh to flourish which supports rare plants and wildlife.

Ⓒ The Western Yar Estuary.

The exposed mud flats make a fantastic habitat for many wetland birds such as Curlew, Redshank, and the elegant Little Egret.

Ⓓ Yarmouth Cycleway.

Formerly a steam railway line this pleasant track has super views across the estuary and is frequented by Red Squirrels, so keep your eyes peeled!

Ⓔ Thorley Old Church.

(Accessible by footpath from the road, FP, Y4.) The original church, built around 1270, was demolished in 1871 leaving just the South porch.

The path can get a little overgrown in the Summer but this adds to the mystery of this little visited spot which is ideal for a picnic.

Nippy Asks:

2. Yarmouth pier is the only one in Britain constructed completely from wood, can you guess how long it is?

An excellent family option, this quiet cycleway offers a traffic free, nature filled excursion into the heart of the countryside. The section from the start to point 6 is known as 'The Troll Trail'*, adding character to this rural route. At various points sculptures and information boards crop up. The section from 7 to 9 is on roads, although very light on traffic, and offers a chance to enjoy a 'loop' before returning to the start. The route is part of Sustrans National Cycle Route 23.

* The Troll Trail was conceived by Gift to Nature who commissioned the Sculptures and nature signs along the route. **www.gifttonature.org.uk** Also check out Gift To Nature's excellent Rail Rides Booklet and The Sunshine Trail.

Start. The cycle path at Shide.　SZ 50355 88103

S Starting from Shide proceed along the cycleway towards Blackwater (signpost 'Sandown 8, Route 23)

1 Just past the troll sculpture and bench, turn L crossing the small bridge and continue to the white gates at Blackwater. Carefully cross over to the white gates opposite.

2 Turn L at the sign 'Sandown 6 ¼, Route 23'.

3 Bear left at this junction (sign, Route 23).

4 Turn L at this junction (sign, Route 23).

5 At the white gates turn R onto the wooded section of the cycleway.

6 When you meet Merstone Lane carefully cross over (follow route 23 sign) and at the next set of white gates take the track to the right of the large sign 'Cycleway & Footpath'. This raised track runs parallel with the cycleway up to the bridge.

7 After emerging onto East Lane (there is a semi-detached house directly opposite) immediately turn L, continue over the bridge and follow the lane.

8 At the crossroads (bridleway A3 on your right) turn L, and at the next junction turn R into Merstone Lane (take care, main road) and after about 350yds/320m, turn L into Chapel Lane (sign, dead end) Take care, Chapel Lane is often used by agricultural vehicles.

9 You will see Merstone Manor (private house) on your right, follow the track to the left, keeping the farm buildings on your left. You will soon will soon pass point 5 and then retrace your route back to the start, following the signs for Newport.

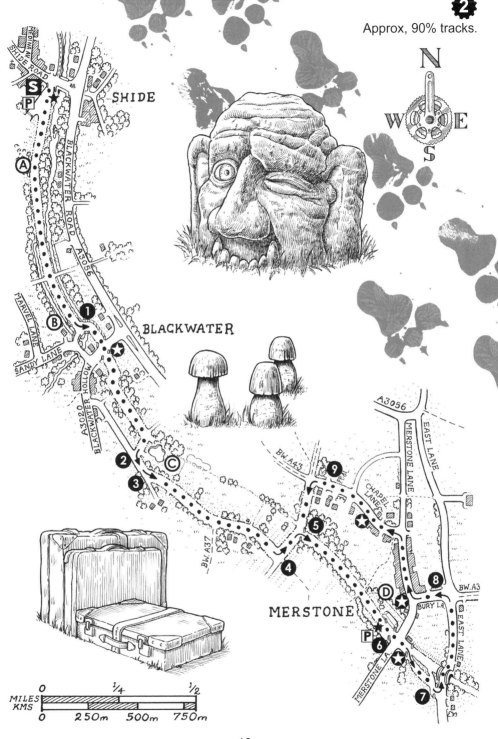

N
W E
S

SHIDE

MEDINA ROAD
SHIDE ROAD

S
P
★

BLACKWATER ROAD

A3056

A
B

1

MARVEL LANE

SANDY LANE

A3020 BLACKWATER HOLLOW

BLACKWATER

★

2
3

C

BW A43

BW A37

MERSTONE

9

5

4

A3056

MERSTONE LANE

EAST LANE

CHAPEL LANE

★

D
★

P
6

BURY LA.

8

BW.A3

EAST LANE

MERSTONE LA.

★

7

MILES
KMS

0   ¼   ½

0   250m   500m   750m

13

POINTS OF INTEREST

Ⓐ Milne's Tree.

Just along the track, there are three small trees on the right, just after these you will find a small plaque on the ground dedicated to Professor John Milne. He is regarded as the father of seismology and studied earthquakes from his nearby observatory in the late 1890s.

Ⓑ Troll sculpture.

Why not think up a name for the troll while you sit on the bench and have a bite to eat?

Ⓒ Birchmore pond.

Just off to the left is a field accessible to the public and the pond has some seating around it, an ideal place to see dragon flies darting over the water.

Ⓓ The site of Merstone station.

Only the platform remains of the original station which closed for good in 1956. It is now very popular with picnickers who make use of the wonderful carved benches.

Nippy Asks;
3.I'm a Red Squirrel, do I hibernate?

A Red Squirrel.
This beautiful little
creature is only found
in a few locations
around the UK. It has
a distinctive 'rusty'
red colouring and at
8inches/20cm high is
slightly smaller than its
grey cousins.

A. Rowe

A ride of potentially two parts. From the start to point 2 there is busy traffic but from 2 to 3 including Puckpool Park is a flat, traffic free, cycle route ideal for the young family. From Puckpool to point 5 it continues to be flat and has light traffic to Seaview. The young family, having explored Seaview may want to turn back at this stage as from point 6 the route has a mixture of off-road and roads with hills and traffic, some of it busy

These hovercraft are part of the world's longest commercial service having started in the 1960s.
The hovercraft itself was first tested on the island in 1959 and was invented by Sir Christopher Cockerell.
See them just after the start point.
The current service is run by Hovertravel (see directory)

The children's play area at Puckpool Park is great fun!

15

Approx, 15% tracks.

Start. Western Gardens.   SZ 59306 92935

S With the pier entrance behind you and facing the various arcades, turn L, proceeding in an Easterly direction, soon passing the Ice Rink and Pavilion on your left.

❶ Turn L at the Canoe Lake (sign, Appley Tower) and at the next junction turn L (sign, Appley Park).

❷ When you reach The Seashell Restaurant and Grill, turn L onto the cycleway (cycle sign, Seaview, please take care, this path is shared by walkers).

❸ As you approach the next cafe (Dell Cafe), bear R into Puckpool Park (cycle sign Seaview). Make your way through the Park (former gun battery), following the one way system and just before the cafe/bar turn L to the left of the Cafe Bar building. You'll encounter a narrow path then turn R at the hedge and through the railings, heading for 'the sea' onto Springvale Rd.

❹ Continue along 'The Duver'. Very soon on your left you will see a large upright stone and some modern granite benches, ideal spot to view the Solent.

❺ Bear R into Salterns Rd. After a short distance you will see a sign 'shops and seafront', follow the road to the R of this sign.

At this point if you want a flat 'family route' you can turn back and retrace your steps back to the pier (when you reach the canoe lake, travel on the left side of the lake and at the small roundabout bear left and turn right back onto the main road). Of course, you can always explore Seaview before returning. This option will give you a total distance of around 2.3miles/3.6kms.

❻ To continue on the main route follow Salterns Rd and then turn R (sign, Salterns Holidays) on bridleway R95 and after 90yds/metres, take the gravel/grass track just to the left of the entrance to Salterns (a wooden fence runs to the left of the track). Climb up the track and at the road (take care here) turn L and continue through Nettlestone. At the village green follow the sign to St Helens, continue along the road passing the village stores on your right. Proceed along Eddington Road to the old church, seen on your right, and after a short distance you will see a sharp bend sign and bridleway on the right (Sign, Attrills Lane, BW R63).

❼ Turn R into Attrills Lane (taking great care when crossing over on the bend!), proceed along the gravel track.

8 You will come to a junction of tracks with a telegraph pole directly in front of you, bear right on the grassy/chalky/gravel track leading downhill. Continue on the track and as it levels out bear left, climbing up the hill.

9 As you approach the barns, bear left then immediately turn R passing the farm house on your left and through the stone gates. Continue on the track, gravel becoming broken tarmac.

10 At the good tarmac road (old stone built house opposite) turn R and at the next junction turn L onto Bullen Rd (no signpost), after descending and then climbing again, cross straight over at the traffic lights and take the next L down Smallbrook Lane (sign, Brickfields Horse Country).

11 Towards the bottom of the hill you will see a 'humped bridge' sign, the right turn you want is directly in front of the bridge and traffic appears quickly over the bridge! It is well worth pulling in to the left, dismounting, and walking with your bike across the road when it's clear. Just before the bridge is a gravel track on the R (sign, Bridleway R54), continue on this.

12 When the track reaches the car park turn R through the wooden gate, up the short section of road and take the next L (into Cross Street, no sign), follow the road and at the next T junction turn L down the hill. Take the next on the right into St Johns Wood Road, at the next T junction turn L into Park Road (sign, weak bridge), continue over the railway bridge and at the T junction turn R into Monkton Street. Proceed for about 400yds/metres.

13 As you approach the shops, turn L into East Street. At the give way sign turn R and then L at the roundabout. Continue to the start at the pier.

Nippy Asks;
4. From point 4 you can see the Spinnaker tower in Portsmouth. How tall is the tower?

POINTS OF INTEREST

Ⓐ Ryde Harbour Area.

From the sea wall there are excellent views of the hovercraft, the worlds longest running commercial service. The Planet Ice Rink and L A Bowl, along with the Peter Pan Playground, make the area a magnet for visitors.

Ⓑ Ryde Canoe Lake.

If you grow tired of riding a bike try pedalling a giant swan!

Ⓒ Appley Tower.

Built as a folly in Victorian days this enchanting tower is currently a shop and for a small fee (refundable with a purchase) you can climb to the top for a fine view of the Solent.

Ⓓ Puckpool Park.

Originally a gun battery dating from 1861, this park has many attractions including putting, tennis, tea and cake.

Ⓔ Seaview Wildlife Encounter www.seaviewwildlife.com

A small detour up the hill (Oakhill Road) will take you to this super collection of creatures including Pelicans, Penguins and Meerkats! Lots to see and do. Open from Easter to the end of October.

Ⓕ The Alan Hersey Nature Reserve.

A pleasant area to walk with a wide variety of bird life.

Ⓖ Seaview Duver Coast Protection Scheme.

In 2003 the sea wall was reconstructed to prevent the risk of erosion and flooding. The elevated walkway, benches and cycle rack make it an ideal place to stop and admire the busy Solent.

Ⓗ Seaview Village.

An attractive village with an active sailing scene. Seaview Yacht Club have regular races off the shore, often using their own fleet of keel boats known as Mermaids.

Ⓘ Fairy Hill.

Legend suggests that in 1545 an attack by the French was driven back by archers hidden in these woods!

Appley Tower

This is an all on-road route which takes you on an undulating journey along generally quiet rural lanes that typify the Island's country road network. There is a route option to visit the 'chocolate box' scene at Winkle Street, ideal picnic and photo territory.

Start. Newtown Old Town Hall.   SZ 42387 90621

S From the Town Hall proceed North, pass the houses and bear right along Town Lane. Follow the road and at the next junction (there is a grass triangle with signs) turn R (sign Shalfleet), and immediately L into a lane (Underwood Lane), there is a slippery surface sign. At the A3054 (busy road) turn R and immediately L into Pound Lane (sign for Five Houses).

❶ At Pump Lane (no lane name but a sign 'Gate Across Road') continue to follow the road to the right, at the next junction turn L (sign to Calbourne) and after a while climb the steep hill to Calbourne.

❷ At the crossroads you can take a detour to Winkle Street (*to do this, go straight over the crossroads, into Lynch Lane and take the second R at the grass triangle. To get back on the main route, retrace your steps back to the crossroads*). If you don't wish to detour turn R at the Sun Inn (this is a busy road), follow the sign to Freshwater and take the next R to Newbridge (no road name but a sign, "6'-6" Except for access").

❸ Follow the road and as it descends to the right look out for the white railings of the bridge, bear L and climb the steep hill into the village. Stay on this road for about ½ mile/800m, and Turn L at the next junction (sign Brook) into Dodpits Lane.

❹ At the main road (this can be busy) turn R , sign for Freshwater/Totland, after climbing a short hill, look out for a thatched cottage on the right as you descend, and take the next right (there is no road name but a sign saying "6'-6" Except for access") (*From point 4 if you wish to visit Chessell Pottery simply cross straight over the junction and you will soon find it on your right. To re-join the main route retrace your steps to the main road*)

❺ Turn R at the next junction, sign to Wellow.

❻ At Wellow (don't follow the sign for Wellow Institute) take the second on the R by the quaint thatched cottage into a small lane (Coopers Lane), over the rustic bridge (probably best to walk over this one!), and turn L at the top of the lane.

Proceed on Wellow Top Road turning L at the next junction into Station Road.

❼ Turn R into Warlands Lane, sign for Shalfleet, and follow the lane until you reach the junction with the A3054 .Turn R here, sign for Newport (Take care at the traffic lights).

❽ Turn L at Shalfleet Garage and into Corf Rd.

❾ At the junction with Town Lane turn L and back to Newtown (sign for Old Town Hall).

Nippy Asks;
5. What is the old meaning of the name Shalfleet?

Newtown Old Town Hall

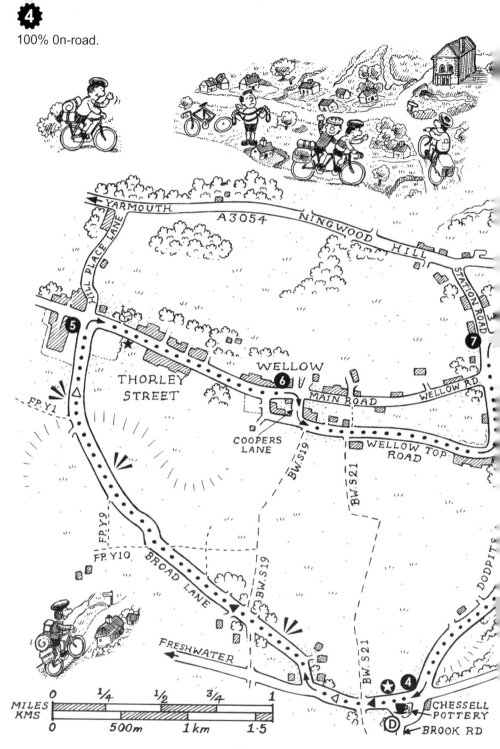

4

100% On-road.

YARMOUTH

A3054 NINGWOOD HILL

HILL PLACE LANE

STATION ROAD

5

7

THORLEY STREET

WELLOW

6

FP.Y1

COOPERS LANE

MAIN ROAD

WELLOW RD.

BW.S19

WELLOW TOP ROAD

BW.S21

FP.Y9

FP.Y10

BROAD LANE

BW.S19

DODPITS

BW.S21

FRESHWATER

BW.S21

4

CHESSELL POTTERY

D

BROOK RD.

MILES
KMS

0   ¼   ½   ¾   1

0   500m   1 km   1.5

24

POINTS OF INTEREST

(A) Newtown Old Town Hall. www.nationaltrust.org.uk/main/w-oldtownhallnewtown

Once The Island's capital Newtown was attacked by the French in 1377 and never recovered. The Old Town Hall dates from the 1690's and is in the care of the National Trust, along with much of the surrounding land.

(B) Winkle Street.

A very pretty scene, much visited and photographed. Ideal for a picnic or a rest.

(C) Calbourne Water Mill. www.calbournewatermill.co.uk

A short detour from the route will take you to the only working water mill on the Island, mentioned in the Domesday Book. It is also a rural museum set in 10 acres of lovely grounds. Open March - November.

(D) Chessell Pottery. www.chessellpotterybarns.co.uk

A working pottery, decorating studio and the 'Ultimate Island Cream Tea'.

(E) Shalfleet Quay.

When passing through Shalfleet (at the traffic lights) why not turn left at the pub and follow the lane (mostly chunky gravel) to the old quay. Lovely spot for picnics or gazing across the water.

*Calbourne
Village Pump*

This route is on-road with a section (1mile/1.6kms) of hard packed gravel track, popular with walkers and cyclists. There is a brute of a hill just after point 1 and to the West of Bembridge Down also a pull up to St Helens (points 5 to 6), otherwise an undulating ride. The B roads are fairly busy, the alternative from point 3 is less so. The ride along the Embankment gives great views of the harbour and its interesting collection of houseboats.

St Helens Old Church at The Duver.

27

5

Approx, 7% tracks (7-8).

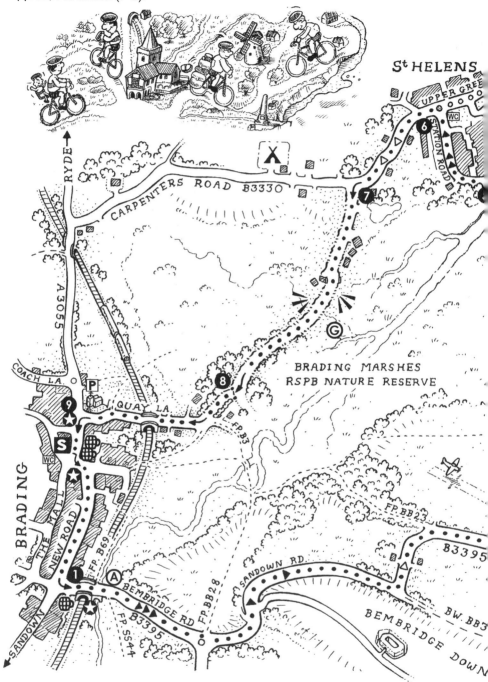

SEAVIEW

DUVER RD.

THE DUVER

F

WC

S⁺ HELEN'S FORT

E

N
W E
S

BEMBRIDGE
POINT

DUNES

D

P

WC

CAUSEWAY

BEMBRIDGE
HARBOUR

EMBANKMENT ROAD

CHURCH RD.

HIGH STREET

FORELAND ROAD

BEMBRIDGE

LANE END ROAD

RNLI
LIFEBOAT

P

WC

C

STEYNE RD.

EGERTON RD.

WALLS RD.

CROSSWAY

FORELAND RD.

FORELAND

MILL RD

B

BW.BB36

4

REC.

BROOK RD.

HOWGATE ROAD

BEMBRIDGE
AIRPORT

HILLWAY RD.

3

FP.BB2.1

HILLWAY RD.

AMONWOOD
LANE

FP.BB18

2

FP.BB.26

WHITECLIFF BAY

CULVER
DOWN

MILES
KMS

0   1/4   1/2   3/4

0   500m   1km

29

Start. The Bull Ring.   SZ 60586 87066

S From the Bull Ring, with Brading New Town Hall behind you, cross over to the Wheatsheaf Inn (take care, busy road) then bear left round the corner. Continue on the main road until you reach the traffic lights at the 4 way junction.

❶ Turn L at the lights and cross the bridge (take care, bridge narrows). Continue on Bembridge Rd and climb the very steep hill to the mini-roundabout, go straight across and continue down the hill (sign, Bembridge B3395).

❷ Just past the Propeller Inn turn R at the triangular grass island (sign, Hillway Road). Follow the road for about 1 mile/1.6 kms, and at the junction with Howgate Rd bear L (sign, Bembridge).

❸ *For an alternative route, visiting the lifeboat station and beach, turn R into Howgate Rd (sign, Forelands) Take the 3rd road on the left, Egerton Rd and at the T junction turn R into Lane End Rd. From the beach retrace your steps, passing Edgerton Rd and continue past the row of shops on your right. At the next junction turn R (sign Bembridge Village Centre). At the next junction follow the one way system to the left and turn R past the church (Church Road).*
If you don't want to take the alternative route, bear left at point 3, sign Bembridge.

❹ Cross straight over at the mini-roundabout into Mill Rd. Continue along the High Street, and bear left at the war memorial on the one way system. Just past the garage bear left at the cycle sign, ride down the hill and continue along the embankment.

❺ *At this point if you wish to visit The Duver follow these instructions, otherwise climb the hill to point 6 now. (Please be aware that this route has a narrow causeway over water and is not suitable for children). At the traffic island (there is a big anchor on it!), turn R into Latimer Rd, after 150yds/metres turn R (there is a street light attached to a wooden pole) then immediately L (look out for signs Coastal Footpath R108). Please dismount and walk with your bike from here. Pass over the stone quay and bear right (sign R86, Public footpath) and follow the route between the buildings. You will now see the causeway. (Take extreme care here for obvious reasons! If you have any doubts, now is the time to turn back. Be aware, there is a short, narrow section about 15 feet long, halfway along which can be under several inches of water at very high tides!). After crossing the causeway turn R, make your way along the well worn path at the waters edge, and turn L at the tarmac road (a stout wooden post marks this place).*

You can now get back on the bike! Follow the road for about ½ mile/800m and to visit the Old Church/ beach turn R at the sign, otherwise bear left and cycle up the hill (Duver Rd). At the top of the hill bear left at the junction into Upper Green Rd, keeping the green on your left, and re-join the main route at the mini-roundabout (point 6).

6 To continue on the main route from point 5, ride straight ahead, climbing Station Rd and at the mini-roundabout turn L (sign, Brading).

7 As the descent flattens out and bears right there are a couple of cottages on the left, turn L immediately after the second cottage, just before the speed limit signs. Follow the footpath sign, B56 onto the gravel/broken tarmac track

8 When you reach the wooden gate on the right proceed through it. Continue on the narrow track and bear R at the tarmac road. Follow Quay Lane and at St Mary's Church and Old Town Hall turn L onto the High Street (take care, very busy road) and back to the start.

Blackberries. In September these succulent fruit abound on the Island's quiet lanes

POINTS OF INTEREST

(A) World War II Pill Box.

Restored by Bembridge Heritage Society, this Pill Box would have been used to defend the Yar Bridge in the event of an invasion. www.bembridgeheritage.org.uk

(B) Bembridge Windmill.

Owned by the National Trust and built around 1700 this is the Island's only surviving windmill. www.nationaltrust.org.uk/main/w-bembridgewindmill

(C) Bembridge Lifeboat Station.

Established in 1867 this station's crew provide safety for seafarers in the Solent. There is a pleasant beach and cafe nearby. www.bembridgelifeboat.org.uk

(D) Bembridge Dunes and Harbour.

The harbour, an SSSI, is an important habitat for wildlife and salt marsh plants.

(E) St Helens Fort.

Built in the 1860s this unusual sea fort was part of Lord Palmerston's defence plan to protect England from French attack. It is one of four such forts in the Solent.

(F) St Helens Old Church and Duver.

Just the tower of this old church remains, used as a seamark for shipping. The Duver (pronounced dove-er) is managed by the National Trust and is a peaceful area of dunes.

(G) Brading Marshes.

RSPB Nature Reserve. www.rspb.org.uk

Bembridge Windmill

St Mary's Church, Brading and old Town Hall
(incorporating the jail)

Nippy Asks;
6.Brading is an ancient town.
Can you guess when it had the
title of 'Town' given to it?

Starting at Wootton this route has a few ups and downs, no huge hills but a couple of challenging inclines. Around 30% of the ride is off-road, mostly gravel and the road sections are relatively quiet, just a couple of busy crossings and the bridge area at Wootton is always busy.

Start. (Opposite the Sloop Inn) Approach road to Lakeside Park Hotel and Spa. SZ 54531 91820

S Looking towards the hotel you will see a bridge made from red brick with a sign saying 15mph. If you look to the right you'll see a small road turning off to the right, take this. At the sign, Fernhill Park, proceed through the gates and climb the hill on the wide gravel cycle path. If the gates are shut there is an entrance to the right, just behind the boulders. (The private sign applies to the burial ground).

1 When you emerge onto the road, bear left, and at the main road turn L (sign, Newport Route 22). Keep on the main road and after a short distance descend a small slope, as the road levels out look for a set of white gates on the right, just past the bus shelter, turn R through these (sign, Newport, Route 22) and onto the cycle track (former railway).

2 A short distance after cycling under the bridge, there is another set of white gates. Pass straight over the road (take great care when crossing) and continue on the cycle track, (sign, Newport).

3 After 600yds/metres, turn R (cycle sign, Newport), proceed on a short section of gravel to the tarmac road and shortly look for a very sharp L turn (cycle path sign on the left) onto the cycle path running parallel with the main road.

4 When you reach the bus stop dismount and cross the main road going through the bollards, (take care, very busy road) and bear right onto East Cowes Rd. At the junction with the A3021 cross over, taking care, and continue up Alverstone Rd (signs, end of speed limit). Having climbed the hill turn R at the next junction (there is a small grass triangle here) and cycle down Brocks Copse Rd (sign "6'-6" Except for access). Take care at the bottom of the steep hill as you cross the bridge. At the junction with Palmers Rd turn L and continue ahead.

5 The road gives way to a gravel track, continue straight ahead on this track, bearing left at the first junction (there are mobile phone masts here). Stay on the track for 1 mile/1.6 kms, and at the 5 way junction take the second R (not Aldene) onto the tarmac road. At the T junction with the High Street turn L, cycle over the bridge, up the hill and turn R (take care crossing over) into Firestone Copse Rd (large pine tree opposite), Proceed for nearly ¾ mile/1.1 kms along this road.

The track from point 5 can get very, very wet after rain, with large puddles forming in the track undulations! If there has been heavy rain recently and you don't fancy a soaking, bear right into Church Rd, pass the church, turn R onto the road and then L into St Edmunds Walk, picking up the main route at the T junction.

❻ Take a sharp L (sign, Binstead) into Newnham Lane (no road name sign), at the junction with Newnham Rd, turn R (sign, Havenstreet). Continue on the main road to Havenstreet, descend though the village, pass under the bridge and past the IOW Steam Railway on your right and continue up the hill for about 600yds/550m.

❼ Look out on the right for a signpost, Public Bridleway, turn R onto the gravel track. After a short distance you'll pass some buildings on the right, proceed through the gate and keep to the rutted track next to the fence on your right. Go though the next two gates before the farm, and when you get to the farm buildings bear left on the track. Pass the duck pond on your left and bear right up a slight slope on the track.

❽ You will encounter a 3 way junction, turn R (wooden finger post, Bridleway Wootton N12).

❾ Cross the railway tracks, take care when crossing, the trains may be old but they are quite fast and very heavy! Continue along the track for about 1 mile/1.6km and finish back at Lakeside.

Nippy Asks;
7. When did The Isle of Wight Steam Railway at Havenstreet first start operating trains?

6

Approx, 30% tracks.

EAST COWES WHIPPINGHAM RD.

A 3021

ALVERSTONE RD.

BROCKS COPSE RD.

EAST COWES RD.

NEWPORT

A 3054

LUSHINGTON HILL

FP.N214

FP.N11

PARK RD.

STATION RD.

GRAVEL TRACK

CHURCH RD.

WOO

FOOTWAYS RD.

ST. EDNUN

PALMERS RD.

CHURCH RD.

HIGH STREET

WC

PACKSFIELD LANE

WC

5

1

4

3

2

D

E

9

8

FP.N2

BW.N12

SB

BW.N16

```
         0      ¼       ½       ¾       1
MILES ▨▨▨▨▨▨▨▨▨▨▨▨▨▨▨▨▨▨▨▨▨▨▨▨▨▨▨▨▨
KMS   ▨▨▨▨▨▨▨▨▨▨▨▨▨▨▨▨▨▨▨▨▨▨▨▨▨▨▨▨▨
         0    500m     1 km      1·5
```

CO

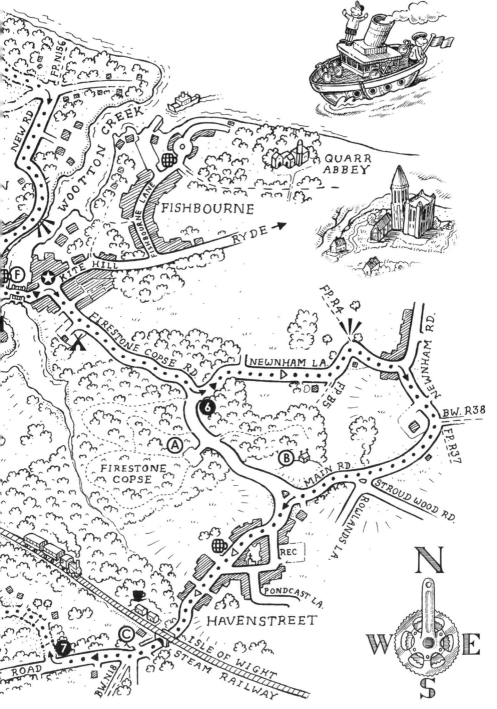

NEW RD.

F.P.N56

WOOTTON CREEK

FISHBOURNE LANE

FISHBOURNE

QUARR ABBEY

RYDE

KITE HILL

B F

FIRESTONE COPSE RD.

FP.R4

NEWNHAM LA.

NEWNHAM RD.

FP.B5

BW.R38

FP.R37

6

A

FIRESTONE COPSE

B

MAIN RD.

STROUD WOOD RD.

ROWLANDS LA.

REC

PONDCAST LA.

HAVENSTREET

C

7

ROAD

BW.N18

ISLE OF WIGHT

STEAM RAILWAY

N W E S

Ⓐ Firestone Copse. www.forestry.gov.uk

Take a small detour to visit this lovely Forestry Commission copse, an ideal picnic spot, look out for those cheeky Red Squirrels.

Ⓑ Havenstreet War Memorial.

This curious shrine commemorates the death of 2/Lt R T C Willis Fleming and others who fell in WW1.

Ⓒ Isle of Wight Steam Railway. www.iwsteamrailway.co.uk

Travel back in time at this living museum and marvel at the beautifully restored steam engines and carriages. Bikes can be taken on the trains. Various opening times during the year, see website.

Ⓓ Briddlesford Fields and Copses.

A pleasant area of parkland with permissive open access, under the Countryside Stewardship Scheme.

Ⓔ Wootton Station.

You can also catch a steam train from here or simply watch them come and go from the picnic benches (the benches are a short walk down the slope from the car park).

Ⓕ Wootton Bridge.

www.woottonbridgeiow.org.uk

A pleasant spot with fine views of the creek and an information board. The shops are a short distance up the High Street.

A Pyramidal Orchid
(Anacamptis pyramidalis)
Look out for this pink or pale purple flower in June and July. The plants height is around 20-45cm/8-18in. It is considered to be the Island's county flower.

In terms of distance this is the longest ride and it takes in a large portion of the 'South Wight', using only on-road routes. It does contain some stiff climbs but also has stunning views from the car park overlooking Blackgang Chine. The route can be made into two shorter circuits by taking an alternative route through Whitwell. Around 30% of the roads can have fairly busy traffic and the route out of Godshill and the Undercliff are popular with visiting drivers.

St Lawrence Well

Nippy Asks;

8. A very famous vegetarian and civil rights campaigner once stayed in Ventnor. Who was he?

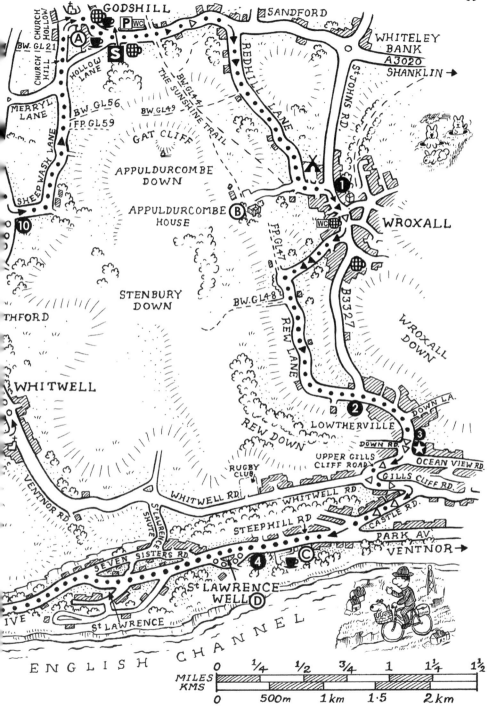

GODSHILL
SANDFORD
WHITELEY BANK
A3020
SHANKLIN →

CHURCH HOLLOW
CHURCH HILL
BW. GL21
A
S
P WC
HOLLOW LANE
REDHILL LANE
St JOHNS RD.

MERRYL LANE
BW.GL56
FP.GL59
BW.GL44 THE SUNSHINE TRAIL
BW.GL49
SHEEPWASH LANE

GAT CLIFF

APPULDURCOMBE DOWN

1 WROXALL

10

APPULDURCOMBE HOUSE
B
WC

FP.GL47

STENBURY DOWN

BW.GL48
REW LANE
B3327
WROXALL DOWN

THFORD

WHITWELL

REW DOWN

2 LOWTHERVILLE
DOWN LA.
DOWN RD.
3
OCEAN VIEW RD.

VENTNOR RD.
St LAWRENCE SHUTE
RUGBY CLUB
WHITWELL RD.
WHITWELL RD.
UPPER GILLS CLIFF ROAD
GILLS CLIFF RD.
STEEPHILL RD.
CASTLE RD.
PARK AV.
VENTNOR →

SEVEN SISTERS RD.
St LAWRENCE WELL D
4
C

IVE
St LAWRENCE

ENGLISH CHANNEL

MILES
KMS
0 ¼ ½ ¾ 1 1¼ 1½
0 500m 1km 1·5 2km

Start. Godshill Car park, opposite The Griffin Pub.
SZ 53001 81687

S From the car park face the Griffin Pub and turn L onto the main road. At about ¾ mile/1.3 kms, turn R into Redhill Lane (sign, 6'-6'' Except for access). When you come to the turning to Appuldurcombe House bear left.

❶ At the T junction with St Johns Rd, turn R (follow the white and blue cycle sign), climb up the hill and then descend past the Worsley Pub on your right and at the bottom of the hill turn R at the stores into West Street. Follow this minor road which becomes Rew Lane.

❷ At Lowtherville emerge onto the main road and bear R (follow the white and blue cycle sign), with the school on your right.

❸ Just past the stores there is a very steep descent, take the second road on the R (sign, Freshwater, take great care when turning right). Descend to a sharp left hand bend (sign for St Lawrence) follow this round to the left (this section has another steep descent). Go through the traffic lights and immediately take a sharp turn to the R, sign St Lawrence. Descend Castle Road and at the junction with Steephill Road turn R (sign for Ventnor Botanic Gardens). Continue for just under 1 mile/1.6 kms to visit St Lawrence Well.

❹ Look out on the left for 3 stone pillars with 2 white gates (see pic opposite). Dismount at the gates and walk with your bike down the path to view the well. To continue on the main route follow the track to the main road. Stay on the road for around 2.2 miles/3.6 kms.

* At the time of writing, the Undercliff Drive, past St Lawrence is closed due to landslides. If this is still the case, turn up Seven Sisters Road, up St Lawrence Shute (very steep hill), and turn left at Whitwell for Niton and to pick up the route.

❺ At this point you will see a road off to the left, St Catherines Rd. *If you wish to visit Knowles Point turn L down this road. Follow the road, passing the Buddle Inn on your right, and look out for Sandrock Road on the right (sign, All Traffic). Bear right into the road and after a short distance turn L into Old Blackgang Rd (sign, Dead End). At around ½ mile/800m the road ends at Knowles Point car park. To rejoin the main route, re-trace back to Sandrock Rd, bear left (follow the one way sign) and then bear left at the next fork (sign, Freshwater).*

To miss out the Knowles Point detour continue on the main road from point 5 and climb the hill (Barrack Shute) to the village.

'3 stone pillars with 2 white gates'

6 At Niton follow the one way system to the left. To continue on the main route go to point 8.

7 *At this point you can opt for a 'short' version of the ride. When you pass the White Lion pub (seen on your right), take the next R into Star Inn Road (sign, Newport). Follow the road round to the right and at the village stores cross over to Rectory Road (sign, Godshill). Stay on this road for 1.2 miles/2 km and at the T junction (an old church on your right) with Ventnor Road turn L (sign Godshill/ Newport). Continue on this road and after 1.5 miles/2.4 km, look out for a R turn into Sheepwash lane (sign, 6'-6" Except For Access). From this point you are back on the main route (point 10).*

8 To continue on the main route from point 6, bear left on Blackgang Rd (sign, Blackgang). There is a long, steady climb to the top followed by a steep descent to Blackgang Chine roundabout (take great care here). At the roundabout turn R and descend to Chale, turn R at the church (sign for Newport), Keep on this road for 3miles/5kms.

9 At the crossroads go straight over into Beacon Alley (sign, Godshill) and take the next R (sign, Roud). At the junction with Whitwell Rd turn R (sign, Whitwell).

10 Take the next L into Sheepwash Lane. Follow the lane and at the junction with Merryl Lane (no sign) bear right passing the 30mph signs. After a short distance bear left at the fork (There are black and white posts and Hollow Lane, no sign, is on the right). As you approach the church turn R down Church Hollow, R at the next junction, through the village, and finally L back into the car park.

POINTS OF INTEREST

Ⓐ Godshill Village.
A very popular location with visitors due to its picturesque appearance and many attractions including museums, tea rooms and even a model village.

Ⓑ Appuldurcombe House. www.appuldurcombe.co.uk
Just off the route are the charming remains of a beautiful 18th century house managed by English Heritage. Also nearby is the Isle of Wight Owl and Falconry Centre with exciting displays. Open 1st April - 30th September, 10am - 4pm.

Ⓒ Ventnor Botanic Gardens. www.botanic.co.uk
A wonderful collection of plants set in beautiful grounds. Enjoy a stroll around the gardens followed by a cuppa'.

Ⓓ St Lawrence Well.
This charming Gothic Revival-styled well was built in the early 1800's. It is seldom visited, tucked away off the main road.

Ⓔ Knowles Point.
In the care of the National Trust, Knowles Point is a hidden gem. Enjoy the rock fallen beauty of the wild scene before you and if you glance up at Gore Cliff there is always the chance of a Peregrine Falcon sighting.

Ⓕ Blackgang Chine. www.blackgangchine.com
Here you will find an amazing collection of attractions set within 40 acres of cliff top gardens. Where else can you sit on a Stegosaurus or walk under a giant smuggler! (Open from the end of March to the end of October)

The 'Pepper Pot', can be seen from the car park above Blackgang Chine. It is the only surviving medieval lighthouse in the UK!

Godshill Church and war memorial

This ride is essentially off-road, with tiny snippets of road. The route is tough going with some narrow, rutted bridleways and a few chain snapping, knee popping climbs! However, the stunning views from the high points at Chillerton Down and Dukem Down are well worth the considerable effort. The surfaces vary from loose gravel to grass and horse hooved mud! So, a short ride but it packs a lot in, testing and rewarding.

The ford and footbridge in Froglands Lane

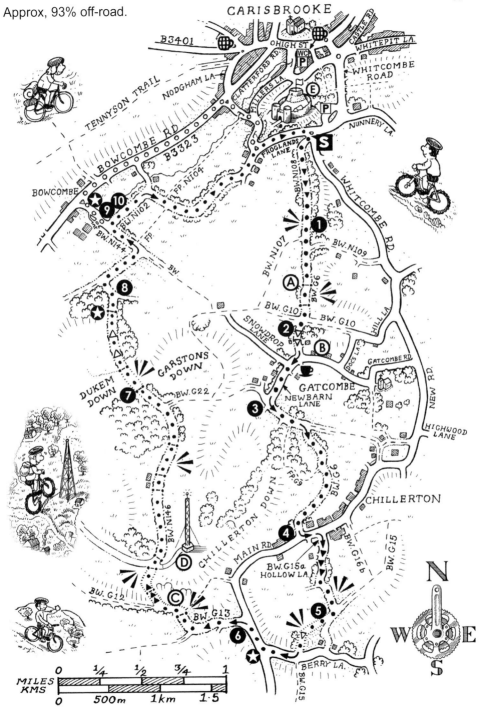

Approx, 93% off-road.

Start. Top of Froglands Lane.   SZ 48748 87427

S From the small grass traffic island at the top of Froglands Lane head South on bridleway N108, Gatcombe.

❶ Having climbed up the steep wooded cutting and emerging on to the flat section you will soon come across a wooden finger post, continue on the trail following bridleway G6.

❷ When you reach the junction with bridleway G10 cross straight over and descend the steep grass track towards the woods (take care very steep and rough surface) when you emerge onto the road there is a bench opposite, turn R and follow the road round to the left (into Newbarn Lane)

❸ When the lane turns sharply to the right, turn L onto the dirt track (sign, G6) Follow the track. Don't take the first turn on the left (farm track) but stick to the worn chalk track going up hill. Continue for 300yds/metres, there is a wooded area on the right, bear left here on the track as you pass the trees and after a short distance (60yds/metres) look out for a hedge on the right, turn R (there is a metal sign post) onto the grass track running along the right side of the hedge. Continue on this grass track to Chillerton.

❹ When you emerge onto the main road turn L and take the 2nd R into Hollow Lane (sign, bridleway G15a). At the top of the very steep climb bear left on the track until you reach 4 signs on a metal pole. *If you wish to cut out this very steep section turn R at point 4 and proceed to point 6, turning R onto bridleway G13.*

❺ The signpost is at the end of a hedge, take the grass track to the RIGHT of the hedge and keeping the hedge on your left proceed along the ridge. After 300yds/ metres, you encounter a bramble thicket, turn L just in front of the brambles down the slope, with the thicket on your right (this is a very, very steep slope, take care on the descent). At the road turn R (take care) and at the next junction turn R.

❻ Turn L onto bridleway G13 and keep on the main track, heading for the mast. Pass through the gate and bear left with the old chalk pit on your right. Ahead of you you'll see a well defined cutting in the grass slope, the track follows this cutting. Pass though the wooden gate and at the top of the super steep climb bear right and go through the gate over the road and onto the gravel track opposite, sign, bridleway N146. Stay on this track.

❼ When you go through this gate you cross open grazing land, proceed down the slope keeping the fence close on your right. There is a very steep drop through the woods just before point 8!

8 As you emerge from the small wooded section bear left, keeping the woods on your left, soon turning R onto the track (there are 2 small yellow discs with blue arrows) continue on the rutted track for 300yds/metres, and at the junction with the next track turn L. As you approach the farm buildings look out for a bridleway on the right, N102. *This bridleway is a pleasant rural track but can get very muddy after rain and is very bumpy, so for an alternative see point 9.*

9 *Instead of turning R into bridleway N102, keep heading towards the farm, cross the farmyard and up onto Bowcombe Rd. Turn R and in about a mile/1500m look out on the right for a grass triangle and sign, Ford, turn R here into Clatterford Shute. After the ford climb a slight hill, bear right and cross the second ford. At the grass triangle, bear L up Froglands Lane back to the start.*

10 To continue on the main route from point 9, turn R into bridleway N102 and follow the track with high hedges on each side. After about one mile/1500m, pass the farm buildings to the right and emerge onto Froglands Lane. Bear right at the grass triangle and climb the hill to the start.

POINTS OF INTEREST

A Mini-cliffs.
Note on your right some mini-cliffs, most likely composed of Cretaceous Upper Greensand laid down around 100 million years ago!

B Gatcombe Village. www.chillertonandgatcombe.org
Mentioned in the Domesday Book this pretty village nestles in a secluded valley and has remained largely undeveloped as there is no 'through road'.

C Old chalk pits. www.nationaltrust.org.uk
These old chalk pits on National Trust land make an ideal location for picnics.

D Chillerton Down Mast.
Erected in 1958, this former TV transmitter now broadcasts radio signals.

E Carisbrooke Castle. www.english-heritage.org.uk
A classic 'old castle' with a moat, towers and slightly ruinous stone walls. It is in the care of English Heritage.

Nippy Asks;
9. How tall is the TV mast on Chillerton Down?

This is an attractive route but very tough! And about 50% off-road. Unlike some of the other rides most of the off-road sections are 'lumpy' bridleways as opposed to smooth cycleways! Having said that, your toil will be rewarded with some delightful countryside not often seen by the average 'tourist'. You could well make a day of this one, stopping for a picnic at point 3 and watching the steam trains, spending some time at Arreton Barns (F) or visiting the Roman Villa (G).

Brading 'New Town Hall' and Bull Ring.

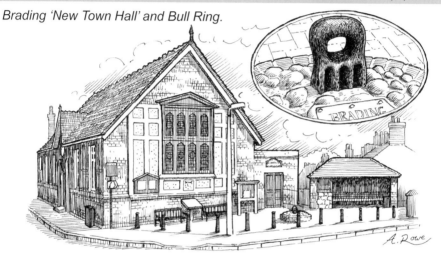

Start. Outside the 'New Town Hall', Brading.

SZ 60586 87066

S Starting at the 'The Bull Ring', face the Town Hall and turn into West Street, with the public toilets on your left. Proceed along the road for around 220yds/ metres and as the road turns sharply to the right, turn L into the narrow lane (Doctors Lane), there are a pair of road signs, motor bike above a car in a red circle (take care, there are two small posts on the lane). *See 14 for off-road start.*

1 As you emerge onto West Lane turn L.

2 At the fork bear L into Ashey Lane (sign, Ashey). At the end of the lane turn L (sign, Newport) then immediately R onto a track (take great care at this junction). There is a sign on the track, footpath R29.

3 Cross the IOW Steam Railway line (sign, Public Footpath R97) and proceed up the lane bearing L at the tarmac road (there are two brick gateposts opposite, and a sign on your left, Station Rd, you have just climbed this!). After around 450yds/metres, look out for a bridleway on the left running alongside a small cemetery (Ashey Cemetery), turn L onto the gravel track (there is currently no signpost, the bridleway runs along the Southern edge of the cemetery). After the very rough track (stones and roots!) go through the gate and keeping the metal water trough on your right (don't take the track to the right of the trough) head down the field towards the lone Oak tree. Proceed past the tree and at the corner of the field is a gate, follow the sign, Bridleway R21 Rowlands Lane, and cross the field keeping the hedge close to your left.

④ Pass the round water trough on your left, and head for the railway line. At the line carefully cross over. In front of you is a hedge stretching across the field, follow the line of the hedge, keeping it close on your left. There are a couple of gaps in the hedge, however, keep going on the same line and when you come to a hedged enclosure keep going ahead with the hedge on your right until you reach 3 trees, and continue onto the gate (there is a telegraph pole next to it). After the gate head for the lone tree straight ahead (very slightly to the right) and through the gate just beyond it. After the gate go straight on aiming for the 2 small trees on the horizon (The right one is slightly dead). At the hedge there is a gate onto Rowlands Lane, turn L at the road.

⑤ At the junction with the main road, cross straight over, sign for Newchurch (taking great care) into Lime Kiln Shute, with its very steep descent, at the bottom bear L, then pass the Garlic Farm on your right. Slow down here and around 400yds/metres past the Garlic Farm look out for an old brick wall on the left (next to sign, Footpath NC1), just after this on the right is a gravel track.

⑥ Turn R onto the track (there is a sign a few metres into the track on the right, Bridleway NC6). Proceed straight along the track, soon passing though a metal gate. Continue for about 1/2 mile/800m to a T junction of tracks (there is a bridleway sign here pointing the way you have just come)

⑦ *At this point you can take an alternative route to visit Arreton by turning R and after 70yds/m turn L (sign, Bridleway A9). Follow the track until you emerge onto the A3056. Turn R onto the main road (in fact you could simply walk with your bike up to the White Lion, Barns and church, on the right hand pavement, it's not far) and take the second R to access the Barns. To return to the main route, travel South East on the A3056 and turn left onto the cycleway at Horringford (cycle sign, Sandown 3, route 23)* To pass on this detour and continue on the main route turn L at point 7, pass several houses on your left and turn L at some old farm buildings (just before Haseley Manor and footpath sign) onto a gravel and old tarmac track, after a short distance turn R onto a chalky bridleway (wooden finger post) and turn L when you reach the cycleway.

❽ At the junction with the road (sign, Langbridge) turn L and immediately R continuing on the cycleway. Travel around 500yds/metres and take the next track to the L (sign, Bridleway Knighton). When you meet the tarmac road (there is a concrete 'hump' onto the road) bear L and at the next junction turn R (place sign Knighton). Proceed for around 440yds/400m.

❾ Turn R onto bridleway NC45, make your way past the buildings and at Harts Ash Farm bear R (small sign, blue arrow on yellow circle) down a wooded track, at the bottom turn L (sign, Bridleway NC45, sign often overgrown).

❿ Cross straight over the road leading to the sandpit and follow byway B35. Go through 4 sets of gates and at Kern Farm (sign, Private) turn R onto a gravel track soon giving way to tarmac.

⓫ Turn L at the junction with the road (there is a grass verge opposite with 3 trees on it).

⓬ Bear R after crossing the 'cobble strip' (sign, Adgestone) Follow the road for the next 2.1 miles/3.4 km, without turning off.

⓭ Cross another 'cobble' strip and at the junction with the main road turn L up a very steep hill, continue straight ahead (signs, 6'6") at the top and descend back to the finish at the Town Hall.

⓮ *There is an alternative off-road route from the start. With Brading New Town Hall behind you, walk on the pavement, with your bike, past the store, keeping it on your right as you go up the hill. When you reach The Mall (30mph signs) cycle up the hill and after about 250yds/m there is a bench and litter bin on your left, just past this on the right is a gravel track (next to Linden Terrace) bridleway B39. Turn R onto the track. Climb the track, soon passing a disused chalk pit on your left and after a steep section keep going until it levels out. Soon after this a track joins your route from the left, continue straight on down the slope. After 900yds/820m, you come to a junction of tracks and a wooden finger post. Turn R, bridleway B59, continue on the track across pleasant parkland, and at the next junction turn L. (see point 2 for next instructions)*

Nippy Asks;
10. Can you guess the year in which the Ashey Down sea mark was built?

POINTS OF INTEREST

(A) Brading Town. www.bradingtowncouncil.org.uk

This ancient town, founded in 1180, holds many interesting attractions including, shops, pubs, an old town hall and quaint church.

(B) Nunwell House. Entrance road just after point 1. www.nunwellhouse.co.uk

Open to the public at various times, Charles the first stayed here on his last night of freedom!

(C) Ashey Down Seamark.

This black and white obelisk was built in the 18th Century and acts as a navigation point for seafarers. This area has its fair share of ghosts, but you don't believe in all that do you...do you?

(D) Isle of Wight Steam Railway. www.iwsteamrailway.co.uk

Why not stop here for a picnic by the level crossing and watch a steam train as it chugs past. In the 1920s hundreds would flock to the annual horse races held in the fields to the South of the crossing.

(E) The Garlic Farm. www.thegarlicfarm.co.uk

THE place for garlic and all things related, with store and cafe.

(F) Arreton Barns. www.arretonbarns.co.uk

A craft village set in a rural location, have a drink, a bite to eat, visit a museum and immerse yourself in countryside tradition.

(G) Adgestone Vineyard. www.adgestonevineyard.co.uk

(H) Brading Roman Villa. www.bradingromanvilla.org.uk

Discovered in 1879 the villa is now protected by a superb modern building. You can gaze upon ancient artefacts then have some tea and cake!

Approx, 50% tracks/off-road.

I.O.W STEAM RAILWAY

ROWLANDS LANE

ROW... WO...

3 TREES

2 TREES

FP.R15

MERSLEY DOWN FP.R16

CHALK PIT

ARRETON DOWN

NEWPORT RD.

LIME KILN SHUTE

MERSLEY LA.

5

9

ARRETON BARNS

ARRETON MANOR

F

THE GARLIC FARM

E

BW.NC6

BW.A9

7

6

KINGSTON LANE

NC4...

BW...

A 3056

ARRETON

HASELEY MANOR

8

ROUT...

ROUTE 23

NEWPORT VIA ROUTE 23
5·2m/8·5km

P

HORRINGFORD

NEWCHURCH
⅓m/·6km

MILES	0	¼	½	¾	1
KMS	0		500m	1km	1·5

54

ASHEY CEMETERY

GATEHOUSE RD

RYDE

DEACONS LA.

LONE TREE

FP.R97

4

D

3

FP.R29

ASHEY RD.

GREEN LANE

ASHEY LANE

HARDING SHUTE

2

WEST LANE

ASHEY DOWN

C

NUNWELL FARM

BW.B59

B

NUNWELL HOUSE

1

COACH LA.

A

P

DOCTORS LANE

S

WC

BW.B32

BRADING DOWN

BW.B39

14

KERN

BW.NC5

BW.B33a

ADGESTONE VINEYARD

G

BRADING

13

10

BW.B35

UPPER ADGESTONE RD.

FP.B44

FP.B49

H

BRADING ROMAN VILLA

MORTON RD.

FP.NC10

11

12

LOWER ADGESTONE RD.

FP.B50

TO SANDOWN
1.5m/2.4 km

This is the hardest of the bunch. It is also potentially very complicated with a few options available. The area ranges from wonderful chalk downland to deep dark woods, so take care when navigating. There is a good mixture of terrain and surfaces including loose gravel, hard packed chalk, grass and compacted mud as well as sections of quiet roads.

There are some very hard and long climbs and some tricky descents! It is perhaps the 'wildest' of the rides in that it takes you though dark forests, over ancient downland and even past a mysterious standing stone (should you choose that route option). Much of the route passes through AONB and Forestry Commission areas.

The Toposcope on Limerstone Down.

Start. The Wilberforce Hall, Brighstone.
SZ 42804 82786

🆂 Wiberforce Hall is almost opposite the Three Bishops Inn and with the Hall at your back turn R and R again into North Street. At the next junction Turn L into Upper Lane and at the next junction (with Moortown Lane) turn R (sign Calbourne)

❶ Look out for a turning on the R (bridleway BS94, Sign, Farm access only) continue on the tarmac, later giving way to gravel, pass the buildings and just after the last house, bear left on the grass track. At the T junction with the next grass track, turn L, then through the metal gate and up the steep climb. After a short distance you will see a wooden sign post.

❷ Turn R, following the sign BS33 and climb up a short grassy slope toward the chalk pit for a few yards onto the bridleway (this can be tricky to find as it makes its way though the scrub). The narrow track then climbs very steeply, with a wire fence on your right, ending in a gate. Near the gate is a sign post, follow BS33 down the slope with the fence close on your right (take care, rutted narrow track) At the next gate on your right stop and pass through it (small yellow arrow), make your way along the top of the ridge with the fence close on your left. Pass through the next gate, go straight ahead up the grassy slope and continue along the top of the ridge.

❸ Yet another gate, with some scrub on the right, pass through the gate and continue ahead along the ridge keeping the gorse on your right, straight ahead and through the next gate, when you reach a patch of gorse, go to the left of it. When you reach the wooden fence posts, bear right down the slope (follow the small yellow pointer, best to dismount, very steep), there is a pond to your right down below, keep the scrub covered slope on your right and look out soon for a gate on the left.

❹ Pass through this gate and continue along the ridge, with the fence on your left and when you come to some old pits, now grassed over, bear R down the slope towards the two nearest houses. When you reach the bottom look out for a wooden sign post and go through the metal gate (Take care, this leads straight onto the road). Turn L at the road, and just past the Crown Inn, turn L at the mini-roundabout (sign Newport). Follow the road round to the left, climb the steep hill going under the wooden bridge.

❺ At the top of the hill take the track on the L (sign, Bridleway SW51). Continue on this steady climb for 1.4 miles/2.3 kms to point 6. (Just past the barn the track becomes mainly grass with two ruts, continue ahead on this until you reach a 'double' metal gate).

❻ Go though the gates and after 100yds/m turn R onto the grassy track (bridleway BS5) heading into the trees. This area has a number of tracks, keep going STRAIGHT ahead!. When you meet the substantial gravel track crossing your path, cross over it (on BS8) and at the next one cross over again (on BS8). Continue for another 500yards/metres.

❼ When you reach a clearing in the woods start to take the track on the right but immediately turn L down a wooded track. Continue along this track and through the gate at the field. Cross the open field keeping the hedge to your left and head for the sea!

❽ At the bottom of the field go through the gate and L onto the track (bridleway CB20, no sign). At the road, Lynch Lane, turn L then soon R onto bridleway CB16b. Stay on this track for 3/4 mile/1200m and just past the farm buildings turn L (there is a small wooden post here with a sign, dogs on leads) and head towards the forest.

❾ At this point the gravel track turns to the right, ignore this and continue STRAIGHT ahead on the grassy track.

10

Approx, 80% off-road/tracks.

B3399

BW.S19

B3401

CHESSELL

BW.S33

⑨

S25

S21

SHALCOMBE
DOWN

⑪

⑩

BW.BS53

Ⓑ

BW.BS89

⑫

BW.S26

BW.CB17

WESTOVER DOWN

BW.BS88

BW.BS44
MOTTISTONE
DOWN

Ⓟ

BROOK ROAD

BW.BS86

BROOK
HILL

BROOK
CHURCH

Ⓒ

THE
LONGSTONE

FP.BS85

STRAWBERRY LANE

⑬

⑭

B3399

BROOK

HULVERSTONE

FP.BS43

MANOR

Ⓓ

MOTTISTONE

BRIGHSTONE

HUNNY HILL

CHILTON LANE

| MILES | 0 | ¼ | ½ | ¾ | 1 |
| KMS | 0 | 500m | 1km | 1·5 |

58

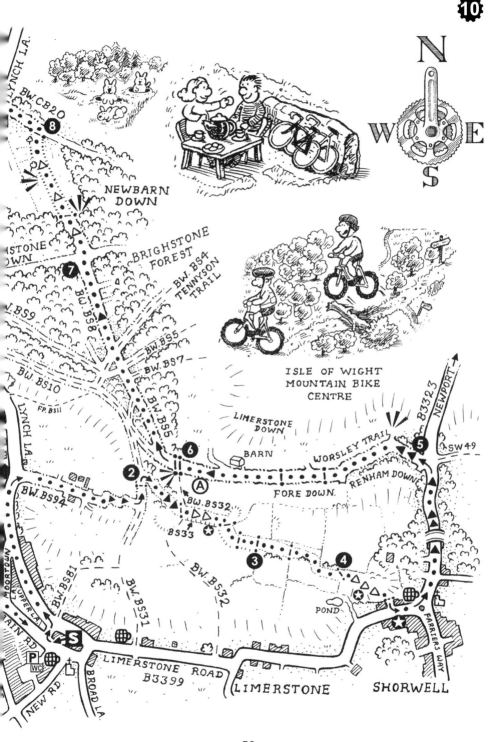

NEWBARN DOWN

BRIGHSTONE FOREST

BW.BS4 TENNYSON TRAIL

ISLE OF WIGHT MOUNTAIN BIKE CENTRE

LIMERSTONE DOWN

BARN

WORSLEY TRAIL

RENHAM DOWN

FORE DOWN.

NEWPORT

B3323

SW49

POND

LIMERSTONE ROAD
B3399

LIMERSTONE

SHORWELL

FARRIERS WAY

LYNCH LA.

BW.CB20

BW.BS8

BW.BS9

BW.BS10

FP.BS11

LYNCH LA.

BW.BS94

BW.BS81

UPPER LA.

MOORTOWN

NEW RD.

BROAD LA.

BW.BS31

BW.BS32

BW.BS5

BW.BS7

BW.BS5

BW.BS32

BW.BS33

10 Enter the woods and bear right following the muddy track. Soon there is a very steep climb and as it levels out keep bearing right. Stay on the gravel track for another ½ mile/800m until you reach a wooden gate, go through this and descend to the road.

11 *At this point you can opt for a tough detour!* (If not, turn L up the hill, see point 12) *Cross the road into bridleway S21. You will soon pass the entrance to a stables on your right, continue bearing left on the track, after a short distance start looking for a SHARP turn on the left (there is a short wooden post on your right with blue arrows and the sharp turn is just before a green junction box on the left). Turn L onto the track and after around 900yds/820m turn L when you emerge at the corner of an open field. Turn L, through the metal gate and up the steep climb (old chalk pit on your right). Keep the woods on your left as you ascend, proceed straight on through another metal gate. After the gate the grassy track gently bears left, after a short distance the fence on your left reaches a corner, when you see this, bear right towards the sea until you meet a track with two ruts in it. Turn L on this track, soon there is a steep, chalky descent which can be slippery when wet, take care. Stay on the track until you reach the road, then turn right to re-join the main route.*

12 *Another possible detour at this point* (if not continue South on Brook Road, to point 14) *turn L, through the gate (bridleway S26, sign,'Except Permits') and climb the steep track. Go though the next gate and proceed up the slope for a short distance until you see a wooden post on your right (sign Tennyson Trail), turn R at this post and immediately turn L (wooden post, sign Bridleway) follow the grassy track and at the old chalk pit (on your left), go though the gate and proceed down the wooded track. At the bottom there is a gate with the caption 'bridle path ends here', and as the sign suggests please walk with your bike on the next section. After the gate turn L, follow the track and you will soon find the Long Stone. With the Longstone at your back and the cottage on your left head down the slope on the worn grass footpath (woods to the right of the path). You pass through 2 gates then on to the road (Strawberry Lane).*

13 *At Strawberry Lane mount your bike, turn R and at the next junction turn L, following the road back to Brighstone.*

14 To continue on the main route, having past past Brook Church on the left and baring left at the bend, stay on the B3399 for another 2.4 miles/3.8 kms back to Brighstone.

POINTS OF INTEREST

Ⓐ Toposcope.

As the track levels out just before point 6, look out on your left for a stone plinth made of chunky flints. On the top is a steel disc engraved with various distances to places as the crow flies including Paris and John O Groats. From here you can see the chalk cliffs at the far east (Culver Cliff) and west (West High Down) of the Island, 21.3miles/34.2kms apart.

Ⓑ Five Barrows.

A group of Bronze Age burial mounds hint at our ancient ancestor's presence in the landscape (If visiting the mounds please walk, as the downland turf is delicate).

Ⓒ The Long Stone.

In the care of the National Trust, this Neolithic standing stone adds an air of mystery to this idyllic landscape. Some say the stones were thrown here by a giant.... I say it's a nice spot for a choccy bar and a sit down.

Ⓓ Mottistone Manor Gardens. www.nationaltrust.org.uk/main/w-mottistone
Maintained by the National Trust these gardens are beautifully presented. Charming walks and a tea garden.

Old wooden footbridge at Shorwell.

🚲 Isle of Wight Cycling Directory

BIKE SHOPS

Al's Bikes. SANDOWN. Unit 8, Senator Trading Estate, off College Close. PO36 8EH. **www.facebook.com/AlsBikes** **T.** 07962373277. Repairs, parts, restorations, custom builds.

The Bike Shed. RYDE . 37 Union Street, PO30 3DL. **www.the-bikeshed.com** **T.** 01983 568833. Bike sales, shoes, helmets, accessories and workshop facilities.

Extreme Cycles. VENTNOR. Church Street PO38 1SW. 01983 852232. Spares. repairs and workshop.

Halfords. NEWPORT. Sales, spares and repairs.Unit 2, Town Gate Retail Park, St James Street. PO30 5HS. **www.halfords.com** **T.** 01983 537182 Bike sales, shoes, helmets, accessories and workshop facilities.

Wight Cycle Works. YARMOUTH. The Old Works, Station Rd, PO41 0QU. **T.** 01983 761800 **www.wightcyclehire.co.uk.** Sales, repairs.

Wight Mountain. NEWPORT. 31, Orchard Street. PO30 1JZ. **T.** 01983 520530 /533445. **www.wightmountain.com** Bike sales, part exchange, shoes, helmets, accessories and workshop facilities.

BIKE SHOPS WITH HIRE

Tav Cycles. RYDE. 140-140a High Street. PO33 2RE. 01983 812989. **WEB.** www.tavcycles.co.uk. Bike sales and hire, shoes, helmets, accessories and workshop.

TOURS

GP Sport. Organised trips and tours, on and off-road, see website for details. **T.** 07733363035. **WEB.** www.gpsport.org

HIRE

Isle Cycle. SANDOWN. Unit 15 Marsh Close PO36 8EU. **T.** 01983 400055 **www.islecycle.co.uk** Free delivery and collection anywhere on the Island. Also have a branch at **COWES.** 1, Terminus Road PO31 7TX . **T.** 01983 299056 Free delivery and collection anywhere on the Island.

Wight Cycle Hire. YARMOUTH. Yarmouth Station PO41 0QT. **T.** 01983 761800 Open 365 days **www.wightcyclehire.co.uk** Wight Cycle Hire deliver to any Island location, have an Island wide mobile support and delivery service.

🚲 Isle of Wight Cycling Directory

ELECTRIC BIKES

Blackman Powerbikes. SANDOWN. Shop, hire and tours.
Unit 6, Lake Industrial Way. PO3 9PL **T**.01983 407049.

LOCAL CLUBS

Autumn Tints Cycling Comrades. www.autumntints.org.uk
A touring club for the over 50s, with a local branch.

Bembridge Wheelers. Leisurely touring from Bembridge. **T.** 01983 872953

Cyclewight. www.cyclewight.org.uk   Local campaign group.

Vectis Roads Cycling Club. www.vectiscc.org.uk
Racing club with Time trials.

The Wayfarer Cycle Touring Club. www.cycleisland.co.uk
Cycle touring and leisurely rides on the island.

Isle of Wight cycling facebook group. www.facebook.com/groups/iowcycletraining
All sorts posted here including events, group rides, information, help etc.

FERRIES / TRANSPORT

Red Funnel. www.redfunnel.co.uk **T.** 0844 844 9988.
email: post@redfunnel.co.uk   Southampton to East Cowes, Vehicle/bike/
passenger ferry. Southampton to West Cowes, Red Jet Hi-speed foot passenger
service.

Wightlink. www.wightlink.co.uk **T.** 0871 376 1000
Portsmouth-Fishbourne, car, bike and foot passengers. Portsmouth-Ryde, foot
passengers/bikes. Lymington-Yarmouth, car, bike and foot passengers.

Hovertravel. www.hovertravel.co.uk **email**: info@hovertravel.co.uk
Southsea to Ryde. Foot passengers only.

Islandline. Trains running from Ryde Pier Head to Shanklin. For times see this
site **www.nationalrail.co.uk**

Southern Vectis. Bus company. **www.islandbuses.info** **T.** 0871 376 1000
This company have some buses on some routes with bicycle carrying capacity,
contact Southern Vectis for detials.

For more specific/detailed information on carrying bikes on any of the ferry/
transport entries please contact the relevant company.

🚲 Isle of Wight Cycling Directory

TOURIST INFORMATION

General Isle of Wight tourist information. www.visitisleofwight.co.uk

Cycling specific tourist information. www.visitisleofwight.co.uk/bicycle-island

EVENTS

The Isle of Wight Randonnee. www.cycleisland.co.uk

An annual 'round the Island' ride of 100 Kilometres (there is a shorter option on the day of 50km). Normally run on the early May bank holiday.

Isle of Wight Cycling Festival. www.sunseaandcycling.com

Hosted by the Isle of Wight Council, this annual event is a week long collection of events from racing to pottering, usually held in mid September.

OTHER

Isle of Wight Mountain Bike Centre. Cheverton Farm, PO30 3JE

www.isleofwightmountainbikecentre.co.uk   A dedicated mountain bike trail centre, open from April - end of September. **T.** 01983 741034

USEFUL CONTACTS

AONB. Isle of Wight Area of Outstanding Natural Beauty. Conserving and enhancing the Island's finest landscapes. **www.wightaonb.org.uk**
T. 01983 823855

CTC. The Uk's National Cyclists' Organisation. www.ctc.org.uk
General enquiries **T.** 0844 736 8450 Membership **T.** 0844 736 8451

Gift to Nature. Undertaking many conservation projects round the Island.
www.gifttonature.org.uk   T. 01983 200074

re-cycle. A charity sending unwanted bikes to Africa.   **www.re-cycle.org**
T. 01983 209090

Sustrans. The UK's leading sustainable transport charity.
www.sustrans.org.uk   T. 0845 113 00 65

Isle of Wight County Press. The Islands weekly paper for news and events.
123, Pyle Street, Newport, PO30 1ST. **www.iwcp.co.uk   T.** 01983 521333

Wight Squirrel Project. An independent local charity and mine of information on red squirrels. **www.wightsquirrels.co.uk   T.** 01983 611003

Nippy's answers. 1.Curlew, Oystercatcher, Little Egret, Redshank.
2.609 ft/185m 3.No. 4.557ft/170m. 5.Shallow stream. 6.1180. 7.1971.
8.Mahatma Gandhi. 9. 751ft/228m 10.1735.